WITHDRAWN

UNIVERSITY OF MINNESOTA

Henry Wadsworth Longfellow

BY EDWARD L. HIRSH

UNIVERSITY OF MINNESOTA PRESS · MINNEAPOLIS

Printed in the United States of America at
Jones Press, Inc., Minneapolis

3 2

Library of Congress Catalog Card Number: 64-63340

Distributed to high schools in the United States by
McGraw-Hill Book Company, Inc.
New York   Chica   Madera, Calif.   Dallas

PUBLISHED IN GREAT BRITAIN, INDIA, AND PAKISTAN BY THE OXFORD
UNIVERSITY PRESS, LONDON, BOMBAY, AND KARACHI

HENRY WADSWORTH LONGFELLOW

EDWARD L. HIRSH is a professor of English at Boston
College. He taught previously at St. Joseph College,
West Hartford, Connecticut.

⌐ Henry Wadsworth Longfellow

THE span of Henry Wadsworth Longfellow's life, from 1807 to 1882, arched over the transforming years between two American worlds. The New England of his birth was agricultural and mercantile in its economy, anchored to seaports, rivers, and farms, provincial but refined in its culture, engaged in reconciling inherited, semi-aristocratic values with the ideals of a circumscribed but dynamic republicanism; the New England of his death was shaped by post-Civil War industrialism, with its noisy railroads, smoky cities and grim mill towns, emerging class conflicts, and crumbling pieties. Of the nature of this transformation, and its real import, Longfellow was, like most of his contemporaries, only partly and at moments aware. To the issues and occurrences susceptible of judgment by his clear, unexamined moral principles or his somewhat vague but deeply felt religious convictions, he responded vigorously — to the "shabby" Mexican War, the antislavery movement, and the human misery caused by financial panics. The range of his interests, however, is clearer in his diaries, journals, and letters than in his poetry. Although his poetry is more frequently topical than is sometimes realized, its relation to the age's history is usually indirect: with some exceptions, events and causes served as catalysts rather than as subject matter or primary topics of the verse. Before many contemporary developments, Longfellow could only confess his bewilderment. Always affective and associative rather than analytic and theoretic in his response to life, he could sense the reality of profound change, and its menace, but he could not criticize

5

it. His characteristic answer was the tireless reassertion of the values cherished by the stable society of his early maturity or drawn from his own love of traditional Western culture and the experiences of his childhood and youth.

Born at Portland, Maine, on February 27, 1807, Henry was the second of eight children, descended from Wadsworths and Long-fellows who had already established their families' provincial importance. His mother, Zilpah, shared his literary interests and inspired him with her own religiously motivated idealism, includ-ing a lifelong hatred of war and violence. His father, Stephen, a public-spirited lawyer, a trustee of Bowdoin College, and briefly congressman from Maine, was an efficient adviser to his son, and later provided him with financial aid as well as encouragement at the beginning of his career. Hardly second to happiness at home was the joy provided by life in a coastal city. The nearby woods and the northward sweep of primeval forest beyond them; the color and bustle of the harbor; above all, the restless Atlantic with its changing moods — these were to haunt Longfellow's im-agination throughout his life and to give much of his poetry its dominant imagery. In his almost obsessive recall of time and hap-piness past, Arcadia lay in childhood and its geography was that of the New England coastline. His most intense poetic exercise in personal recollection is "My Lost Youth," whose familiar third stanza echoes the tone of the whole:

> I remember the black wharves and the slips,
>   And the sea-tides tossing free;
> And Spanish sailors with bearded lips,
> And the beauty and mystery of the ships,
>   And the magic of the sea.
>   And the voice of that wayward song
>   Is singing and saying still:
> "A boy's will is the wind's will,
> And the thoughts of youth are long, long thoughts."

6

In 1821, Longfellow was admitted to Bowdoin College, at Brunswick, Maine, although he did not take up residence there until his sophomore year. Inadequate as the young college was in several respects, its curriculum, modeled on Harvard's, prescribed substantial study of the classical languages, mathematics, scripture, and the branches of philosophy, as well as briefer study of natural science. Longfellow, well prepared by Portland Academy and by his own extensive reading, readily mastered the required subjects and also took the then-rare opportunity to receive part-time instruction in French. As important as his work in course was the informal education he received, especially through his membership in the Peucinian, a literary society with a well-stocked library. The reading and critical discussion of papers at its meetings sharpened Longfellow's growing desire for a literary career. This bias may have been further encouraged by a faculty member, Thomas Coggswell Upham, who came to Bowdoin in 1824 with a missionary zeal for the creation of a native American literature. So well did Longfellow profit from the combined influences of his collegiate years that his academic promise came to the attention of the trustees. In 1825 the new graduate was offered a just-established professorship in modern languages, with the stipulation of a period of European study — at his own expense — as preparation for the position. The offer was quickly accepted, and on May 15, 1826, Longfellow sailed from New York.

The three years in France, Spain, Italy, and Germany were touched with enchantment as Longfellow's romantic imagination responded to a past still visible in monuments and customs, to the storied associations which were, the associationist critics maintained, the source of poetic beauty. Longfellow also laid down solid intellectual foundations, especially in Romance languages and literature, but the new task he envisaged from his steadily American perspective was essentially artistic: to help create a great

7

national literature not by radical novelty, as the so-called "Young American" writers urged, but by transmitting to America a rich European heritage for incorporation into its own culture. His pursuit of this goal through essays, lectures, translations, and adaptations from foreign literature exacted a price: if it did not cause, it certainly intensified the bookish tendency of Longfellow's writings. It also resulted, however, in an important contribution to the increasingly important relationship between American and European literature.

Assuming his professional duties in September 1829, Longfellow discovered that he had virtually to establish a new area of studies and to provide its very materials; between 1830 and 1832 he edited or translated six texts in French, Spanish, and Italian. His labors were rewarded: his competence in basic instruction, skill as a lecturer, and courtesy to students quickly made him an influential teacher. Further, he was making a professional reputation. His translations — the book-length *Coplas de Don Jorge Manrique* appeared in 1833 — attested his linguistic proficiency, in Spanish particularly; he was also publishing essays on southern European languages and literature that demonstrated scholarship. Longfellow's attention in these years was focused primarily on academic achievement; the writing of original poetry, begun before he entered Bowdoin and continued during his college days, had almost ceased after 1825, and his literary ambitions now found outlet in prose sketches of his travels interspersed with tales in the manner of Washington Irving. After an abortive beginning in serial form, the completed account was published in 1833–34 as *Outre-Mer: A Pilgrimage beyond the Sea.*

There were also nonprofessional reasons for satisfaction. After a short courtship, Longfellow was married in 1831 to Mary Storer Potter, a delicately attractive girl interested in mathematics and poetry, who made a self-effacing but effective helpmate. Yet, for

8

Henry Wadsworth Longfellow

all his success, Longfellow found Brunswick distressingly provincial after Europe, and energetically sought a larger public stage. This he attained in 1834, when the distinguished George Ticknor, Smith Professor of Modern Languages at Harvard College, designated Longfellow as his successor. Once more preparatory study abroad, this time in Germanic languages, seemed wise, and the Longfellows left for Europe in April 1835.

The pattern of Longfellow's life was decisively changed by the second European journey. The linguistic goals were accomplished: Longfellow added Dutch, Danish, Icelandic, Swedish, and some Finnish to his store of languages, acquired a thorough knowledge of German romantic literature, and began his lifelong reading in Goethe. It was not intellectual achievement, however, that made the period crucial, but the violent emotional experience originating in his wife's death. Mary's health had always been uncertain; now she was pregnant, and the rigors of a Scandinavian trip exhausted her. Back in Holland, she suffered a miscarriage; infection subsequently developed, and on November 29 she died. Soon after sending her body home for burial, Longfellow received news of the death of his closest friend. Suddenly, it seemed to him, life had taken on the unreality, the transiency, of a dream. Courageously, at times hectically, he pushed on with his work, haunted by loneliness and often acutely depressed.

In the spring of 1836, his spirits slightly improved, Longfellow visited the Tyrol. In July, at Interlaken, he encountered the wealthy Bostonian Nathan Appleton and his family, and with the beautiful, talented, and sensitive young Frances Appleton he fell promptly, passionately in love. In August he had to leave for America, his love unreturned; thus began an extended courtship, long unpromising and broken off by Fanny after publication of the too-autobiographical *Hyperion* in 1839. A chance meeting four years later begot a reconciliation, and on April 17, 1843,

Longfellow received a note from Fanny that set him walking at top speed from Cambridge to Boston through a transfigured day, and into one of the happiest marriages on record.

The seven-year wait, however, was not spent in palely loitering. Occupying rented quarters in Brattle Street's dignified Craigie House, now maintained as a Longfellow museum, Longfellow performed with distinction his duties as Smith Professor. Although he came to detest departmental business and the drilling in fundamentals, and conducted a continuous, low-keyed quarrel with Harvard's then-conservative administrative policies, he took real delight, as did his listeners, in the delivery of his scrupulously prepared lectures. He not only gave the expected instruction in the history of European languages, but opened to his students the world of modern German literature, of Jean Paul Richter, Schiller, and, above all, Goethe. His teaching of *Faust*, indeed, was the first such offering in an American college.

More important to his own future, he also resumed writing, the European experience having reawakened the long-dormant creative impulse. In 1839, in addition to the prose *Hyperion*, there appeared *Voices of the Night*, his first collection of poems, some of which, including the sensationally popular "A Psalm of Life," had been previously printed in magazines. *Ballads and Other Poems* followed in 1841; *Poems on Slavery*, written during his return from a brief third European trip, in 1842; and a poetic drama, *The Spanish Student*, in book form, in 1843. The renewed conflict between academic and literary ambitions was increasingly resolved in favor of the latter, until it was settled in 1854 by the cessation of teaching.

Longfellow's success was already making him a public figure, a role for which he was well suited. Striking in appearance, elegant, even dandified in dress, urbane and mildly witty, endowed with innate courtesy and a peculiarly masculine sweetness of temper, he made the very model of a New England gentleman-author, and his genuine talent for friendship rapidly wove a web of lasting relationships that embraced the obscure and the famous alike. When he and Fanny were married on July 13, 1843, his father-in-law's gift was Craigie House itself, and the young Longfellows soon gave it a wide reputation as a center of cultivated hospitality.

The years from 1843 to 1860 were Longfellow's most fruitful. Besides editing and contributing to three collections of verse, he wrote many of his best shorter poems, gathered in *The Belfry of Bruges and Other Poems* (1846) and *The Seaside and the Fireside* (1850), as well as "Paul Revere" and "The Saga of King Olaf," to be used later in *Tales of a Wayside Inn*; a novel, *Kavanagh* (1849); and his most successful long poems: *Evangeline* (1847), *The Golden Legend* (1851), *The Song of Hiawatha* (1855), and *The Courtship of Miles Standish* (1858). Many of the volumes sold in numbers and with a speed unprecedented in American publishing history.

Public acclaim mounted yearly in Europe as in America, while distinguished guests and unimportant strangers descended endlessly upon Craigie House and seriously hindered Longfellow's work. Moreover, his domestic happiness was nearly complete, shadowed only by the death of one of the six children born to the Longfellows. The single source of continuous anxiety was the national scene. Longfellow observed the sharpening prewar tensions closely and with growing concern, until the opening of hostilities left him torn between his abhorrence of slavery and his hatred of war, and dejected by public disaster.

To national tragedy was soon added personal. On July 9, 1861, Longfellow was resting on a couch in his study while, in an adjoining room, his still romantically loved wife was sealing locks of their daughters' hair in packets: a scene so Victorian as to seem a period piece. Then a spark or a drop of hot wax ignited Fanny's flimsy summer dress. Ablaze and in agony she ran to Longfellow, whose efforts to beat out the flames left him critically burned. During the night Fanny died and, while she was being buried, Longfellow lay helpless in bed, his life feared for, his sanity at first despaired of by his friends and himself. Physically he made a thorough recovery, although the circumstances of Fanny's death had a grotesque consequence: the scars on Longfellow's face made further shaving impossible, and thus was created the placid bearded image that was destined to gaze from the walls of a thousand future classrooms. Psychic recovery came more slowly, and the inner wounds never completely healed. The journals for the following months he later destroyed, but evidence of his near-despair survives in communications with his friends.

To this shattering experience Longfellow directly refers only once in all his later poetry, although knowledge of it is necessary to a full understanding of several poems, including the six sonnets prefixed to his translation of Dante, and the tone of his lyrics is pervasively affected by it. The sole direct reference is a sonnet written in 1879, when Longfellow came upon a picture of a mountain in whose ravines lay a cross-shaped deposit of snow, and found there the image of his unrelenting pain:

> In the long, sleepless watches of the night,
>   A gentle face — the face of one long dead —
>   Looks at me from the wall, where round its head
>   The night-lamp casts a halo of pale light.
> Here in this room she died; and soul more white
>   Never through martyrdom of fire was led
>   To its repose; nor can in books be read
>   The legend of a life more benedight.
> There is a mountain in the distant West
>   That, sun-defying, in its deep ravines
>   Displays a cross of snow upon its side.
> Such is the cross I wear upon my breast

12

These eighteen years, through all the
   changing scenes
And seasons, changeless since the day she died.

"The Cross of Snow" was published posthumously; like another sonnet, the "Mezzo Cammin" of 1842, it seemed to Longfellow too personal for print.

Initially forcing himself to resume writing as an escape from grief, Longfellow was soon engaged in some of his most ambitious undertakings. The three series of narrative poems constituting *Tales of a Wayside Inn* were published in 1863, 1872, and 1874 respectively; the translation of the whole of the *Divina Commedia* occupied the years from 1865 to 1867; the *New England Tragedies* appeared in 1868 and *The Divine Tragedy* in 1871, two works that were linked with *The Golden Legend* by prologue, interludes, and epilogue to make up the complete *Christus* in 1872. From 1876 to 1879 Longfellow acted as editor, in practice as editor-in-chief, of the thirty-one volumes of *Poems of Places*, which included several of his own contributions. Meantime, a but slightly diminished flow of shorter poems, including the fine sonnets, continued, filling most of six volumes: *Flower-de-Luce* (1867); *Three Books of Song* (1872); *Aftermath* (1873); *The Masque of Pandora and Other Poems* (1875); *Kéramos and Other Poems* (1878); and *Ultima Thule* (1880).

These last years were for Longfellow the years of apotheosis. The distinctions between the poet and the venerable figure of Craigie House were lost in a chorus of affectionate acclaim, in which the dissenting voices of the younger generation were drowned out. The last European journey in 1868–69 was an almost royal progress, with honorary degrees conferred by the universities of Oxford and Cambridge, to the cheers of the undergraduates, and with a reception by Queen Victoria. From the continent, Victor Hugo saluted Longfellow as a man who brought honor to America,

13

and at home the schoolchildren of Cambridge presented him with an armchair made from the wood of the original spreading chestnut tree. In American eyes, he was clearly the uncrowned poet laureate, and he played his part to the end. On March 12, 1882, he finished ten six-line stanzas of "The Bells of San Blas," typically celebrating with nostalgia a past of picturesque devotion when "the priest was lord of the land." On March 15, he also typically added a single-stanza counter-statement:

> O Bells of San Blas, in vain
> Ye call back the Past again!
> The Past is deaf to your prayer;
> Out of the shadows of night
> The world rolls into light;
> It is daybreak everywhere.

He had reassured himself and his readers for the last time. Nine days later, after a very brief illness, he was dead at the age of seventy-five, and the spontaneous mourning was international. Enough uncollected poems remained to provide *In the Harbor* (1882), and, in 1883, the impressive fragment of his projected poetic drama, *Michael Angelo*, was separately published. With this his art had reached its period, a fact emphasized by the substantially complete and massive edition of his works in 1886. In its eleven volumes the results of sixty-two literarily active years were assembled for the judgment of posterity.

Longfellow's prose works are, with one exception, of minor importance. *Outre-Mer* contains vivid descriptions of Western Europe in the 1820's, and reflects Longfellow's romantic sensibility in a charming manner, but its studied picturesqueness palls, and it remains inferior to the *Sketch Book* that it too obviously imitates. Longfellow's various essays and articles, important in their day, are now chiefly of historical and biographical interest. Their knowledge has been superseded, and their critical methods

14

and point of view seem outmoded. The one novel, *Kavanagh,* lacks the technical and imaginative unity necessary to success. Its moderately realistic representation of life in a rural New England community deserves the praise Emerson gave it, and there are some amusingly lively scenes satiric of old-line Calvinism and of the patriotic literary theory that assumed the future greatness of American poetry as a consequence of the greatness of American scenery. The love story, however, is flat and sentimentalized, and the characters are insubstantial, save for the sensitive but ineffectual Mr. Churchill, apparently Longfellow's wry portrait of an aspect of himself. In the end, *Kavanagh's* intention is obscure, its construction feebly episodic. Only in *Hyperion: A Romance* did Longfellow succeed in extended prose fiction.

Hyperion, the most autobiographical of all Longfellow's works, describes under a thin veil of fiction the personal crisis of 1835–36; by Longfellow's own account, its writing was a therapy by which he worked his way from morbidity to health. The spiritual journey, a frequent theme in his works, is imaged here in a romanticized account of the second European trip. Paul Flemming, the hero, despairing over the loss of his "dear friend," retraces Longfellow's expeditions and experiences; at Interlaken he meets and falls in love with Mary Ashburton (Frances Appleton) and is rejected by her. Finally, restored to mental health, he self-reliantly faces the future alone — a stance that his creator and original was unable to adopt. So immediately identifiable were the persons and events of *Hyperion* that "all Boston" was soon happily gossiping and being scolded by Longfellow for its narrow-minded censoriousness. Only as passing years dimmed the topical interest could *Hyperion* be read as an imaginative representation of a not simply personal but generically youthful and romantic odyssey.

Into *Hyperion* Longfellow poured the accumulations of three years. Traveler's notes, long descriptions, general reflections, anecdotes and tales, extended literary and philosophic commentaries, topics from his Harvard lectures, translations from German literature — all are crowded in, often with little explicit connection, and are set in a romantic-plush style certain to try the patience of post-romantic readers. Longfellow was then under the spell of Jean Paul Richter, whose style, in apparent chaos, mingled the serious, comic, sublime, and grotesque; it delighted in abruptly changing moods, materials, and manners, in archaic phrasing, flamboyant figurative expression, and rhapsody. In varying degree, these qualities are also in *Hyperion*, so that the first impression is of confusion and cloying whimsicality. Beneath the patchwork, however, lies a real unity of emotion and experience.

The symbolism of the central journey is developed in simple, traditional imagery. Beginning on a dark, cold, mist-shrouded December morning in the Rhine valley, the action moves, for the climactic scenes of Book IV, up into the Swiss mountains in full summer, with the sun high and strong. The past is figured throughout by darkness and the grave, and is extended to include not only Flemming's personal past but the historical past whose monuments surround him in Europe; similarly, the present is a brightness into which not only he but mankind must enter. As Flemming's enthrallment began at a grave, so deliverance comes in St. Gilgen's churchyard among the tombs. The liberating formula he finds, as Longfellow actually found it, on a tablet affixed to a tomb: "Look not mournfully into the Past. It comes not back again. Wisely improve the Present. It is thine. Go forth to meet the shadowy Future without fear, and with a manly heart."

The immediate result of this directive Flemming calls almost miraculous, but later he asks, "Can such a simple result spring only from the long and intricate process of experience?" The process of a single experience is precisely what unifies, however loosely, the widely disparate materials of *Hyperion* and revivifies its traditional imagery by providing a freshly individual context. Embodying a conflict that runs throughout Longfellow's life and poetry and displaying at length the recurrent terms and images of that conflict, as well as of its outcome, *Hyperion* forms the literary substratum of a large part of Longfellow's later work.

Outre-Mer and *Hyperion* played a significant part in making Europe's thought and art available to the American public; so, too, did Longfellow's translations of poetry, which occupy a substantial place in his canon and were produced with varying frequency throughout his career. To translation Longfellow was drawn by his personal, sometimes indiscriminate delight in European literature, as well as by the literary and linguistic challenge of the task itself and the pedagogical usefulness of the results. Spanish, Italian, and German literature furnished the most numerous originals, but there are also translations from French, Danish, Swedish, Anglo-Saxon, and Latin poetry, and even three renditions, via extant prose translations, of Eastern poems. The originals are qualitatively a hodgepodge of everything from sentimental trivia to Dante's *Divina Commedia*.

Accepting Goethe's belief that the translator should adopt the author's situation, mode of speaking, and peculiarities, Longfellow scrupulously attempted to minimize the unavoidable sacrifices of translation and to move as close to literal correspondence as other considerations permitted. His earlier translations take measured liberties, such as the use of "equivalent stanzas" in rendering the *Coplas de Don Jorge Manrique*; his later translations are austerely restrictive. The great test was the translation of the *Divina Commedia*. After pondering the insurmountable difficulties of Dante's *terza rima*, Longfellow decided to abandon the rhyming so that he could preserve the tercet structure and achieve literal precision. The justification of this decision is the translation itself, which, in spite of unevenness and deficiencies, reflects something of the linguistic economy and rhythmic severity of the original. Although Longfellow's rendition does not attain the semi-independent poetic value of great verse translations, it remains one of the most faithful and effective Englishings of Dante.

On the value of translation to the practicing poet, Longfellow was of divided mind. Judging from his own experience, he insisted that successful translation evidenced real creative power, and that the act of translating served as stimulus to the poet's own thought and feeling; but he also refers to the attendant dangers. Translation is, in his own words, "like running a ploughshare through the soil of one's mind; a thousand germs of thought spring up (excuse this agricultural figure), which otherwise might have lain and rotted in the ground — still it sometimes seems to me like an excuse for being lazy, — like leaning on another man's shoulder." For Longfellow, whose art was highly responsive to external suggestion, translation probably did start ideas, and it undoubtedly contributed to his notable skill in versification. Nevertheless, his preoccupation with translation, during a period of life normally crucial in the development of independence, may indeed have encouraged a habit of leaning on other men's shoulders that partly explains the limited originality of his own subsequent poetry.

Longfellow's first published poem, "The Battle of Lovell's Pond," derivatively celebrating a skirmish whose importance was monumentally local, appeared in the Portland *Gazette* for November 17, 1820, over the signature "Henry." Between this and the final "Bells of San Blas" stand well over five hundred poems whose variety makes generalization pause. Ranging from such brief, pure song as "Stars of the Summer Night" to the composite *Christus*, which occupies one hundred and sixty double-columned pages in the Cambridge Edition, the poetry includes not only "ode and elegy and sonnet" in abundance, but hortatory, meditative, and imagistic lyrics; poetic dramas; and many kinds of narrative from popular ballad to epic-tinged idyll, of widely varying length and manner. The gamut of quality is almost as extended, the good poems being sometimes obscured by the disproportionately large number of bad or indifferent ones. Some lines of development can be chronologically traced, especially for the long poems, but these, with rare exception, mark tonal and emphatic changes, or shifts in predominant verse forms or genres, rather than fundamental alterations in Longfellow's major ideas or attitudes, which, although modified with time, persist in recognizable form from *Voices of the Night* to the end.

The essential characteristics, even the qualitative variance, of Longfellow's poetry are related to his humanistic although unsystematized views on art. Art, he held, is the revelation of man, and of nature only "through man." His abandonment of nature-description, Longfellow explained, meant not that he loved nature less, but man more. This basically traditional attitude receives a distinctively nineteenth-century coloring from Longfellow's understanding of artistic usefulness in terms of "elevation." Poetry, he argued in his 1832 "Defence of Poetry," is an instrument for improving the condition of society and advancing the great purpose of human happiness; in America's democratic society, this implied an endorsement of literature's growing concern with the literate common man. Longfellow's Michael Angelo, in the drama bearing his name, defines art as

> "All that embellishes and sweetens life,
> And lifts it from the level of low cares
> Into the purer atmosphere of beauty;
> The faith in the Ideal . . ."

Thus poetry, even at the risk of losing itself in the "low cares," will serve to charm, to strengthen, and to teach — a formula in which many critics and poets concurred: Walt Whitman, praising Longfellow as an unrecognized master in the treatment of com-

19

mon occurrences, declared his evocation of the poetic quality of everyday things to be truly representative of the spirit of democracy.

That a useful muse might become too housewifely Longfellow was aware. The nature and the problems of the artistic process make a recurrent theme in his poetry, especially from the two poems "Prometheus" and "Epimetheus" of 1854 to the poems of the 1870's, *The Masque of Pandora*, "Kéramos," and *Michael Angelo*, and the problem most reflective of his own experience was that of the frustrating distance between the exaltation of original inspiration and the flatness of final achievement. Longfellow knew that the highest inspiration is Promethean, and he suspected that great art comes only from the continual isolation and the total commitment of struggling with the gods — the art of a Shakespeare or Dante, before whose accomplishment he openly confessed his own inadequacy. Yet, like many of his contemporaries, he half-feared this heroic posture as a humanly perilous one, a cutting-off of the artist from humanity's common lot, from the world of Pandora's opened box and Epimetheus' humanitarian compassion. How the initial lofty vision could without betrayal and without obscurity be made accessible and instructive to a wide audience was the puzzle. Finding no solution, Longfellow accepted without undue repining the Epimethean role of poetic concern with daily sorrows and hopes, but he was haunted by the figure of Prometheus, symbol of the daring act of imagination essential to the birth of all poetry, even that which apparently ended up in slippers at the fireside.

The major ideas underlying Longfellow's poetry are characteristically expressed in a conventional nineteenth-century terminology that invites partial misreading, partly because of subsequent changes in meaning, especially in connotation, and partly because important terms are often so inclusive as to seem indeterminate. Longfellow's constant appeal to the heart is frequently understood as the consequence of a vague, sentimental notion that the gentler emotions could resolve problems and order life, to the near-exclusion of thought. His usage, however, like that of his contemporaries, reflects an older and wider meaning of *heart*. The word refers not only to the emotions, but also to will and intuitive reason. When Longfellow writes,

> "It is the heart, and not the brain,
> That to the highest doth attain . . ."

his use of "heart" is close to that of the Pauline formula, in the phraseology of the Authorized Version, "with the heart man believeth to righteousness." The heart, therefore, may stand for all of man's immaterial nature, save his discursive reason, which is often signified by "brain." Moreover, in his simple division of man into body and soul, Longfellow assigned all thoughts, all feelings, all desires to the soul, not the body, which is only the instrument. "It is the soul," he insisted, "that feels, enjoys, suffers . . ." Thus the affections themselves are spiritual, and, directed to good ends, can properly be called "holy."

Longfellow's frame of ultimate reference is formed by his religious convictions. When he established in 1824 the first Unitarian society at Bowdoin, he was not simply revolting against the "consocation of 'old sanctities,'" as he once called the college's conservatively Congregationalist clergy, but affirming the strong personal faith that pervaded his life and writings. Like his father, Longfellow in general accepted the teaching of William Ellery Channing: that man is fundamentally good, endowed by God with reason, conscience, and an intuitive awareness of the divine; and that Christianity, the purest faith known to man, is progressing toward a full realization of its ideals in a universal church of the future. The core of man's religion is a self-sacrificial love issuing in noble actions and sentiments, and in humanitarian concern for human welfare. Not by creeds, whether Athanasian or Calvinistic, but by deeds is man judged, and his faith made effective.

For so optimistic a belief, the chief problem is that of sin and evil, and the greatest imaginative failure of Longfellow's poetry is its inability to probe life's dark or sordid aspects. The causes of failure were partly temperamental. A natural fastidiousness led Longfellow to recoil from the physical and spiritual ugliness that caused him actual pain. Although he was personally subject to periods of neurotic depression with moments of panic, he regarded these visitations as transient phenomena that raised no intellectual question about man's nature or destiny. What experience failed to provide, faith could not supply. Especially in his long poems, Longfellow represents or alludes to the malicious, fanatic, and selfish behavior men are capable of, but he suggests no deeper cause than a defect incidental to man's present condition, reformable although not yet reformed. The chief weakness of *The Golden Legend* is therefore the characterization of Satan, who, although cast as a fallen angel, is in action only a badly behaved, treacherous superman, neither terrifying nor awe-inspiring, and almost cursorily dismissed. Somehow — and Longfellow is never deeply curious about "how's" — everything will come out all right. So, at least, his reasoning assured him. Yet his attraction to Dante, the pessimistic feeling that tinges *Christus*, and the powerful vision of final nullity in *Michael Angelo* all suggest a sensibility whose perceptions are often at variance with the formulating ideas.

The simply held ideas by which Longfellow attempted to order experience are frequently unable to contain the strong current of feeling that is a distinctive quality of his romantic sensibility. Although he was sharply critical of what he considered the excesses and absurdities of romanticism, his own poetry is saturated with a romantic sense of life's fragility. The crumbling ruins, encroaching darkness, and vivid but fleeting visions are not fashionable accessories, but the authentic images of Longfellow's deepest emotion, as his journals testify. That human life is a dream in which the apparent solidities of time and place dissolve into insubstantial forms is a nearly obsessive theme. To Longfellow, the most powerful flow of time and consciousness is backward, from present to past, from actuality to dream, and into the magic night of communion and reminiscence that gives access to the remembered past. However tempered in expression by his almost classical restraint and social poise, the dominant mood of Longfellow's poetry is a melancholy not unlike that of Washington Irving, compounded of nostalgia, the sadness of personal loss, and the painful awareness of transience and mortality. If there is truth in the comment that Longfellow did not face the primary facts of life and nature, one reason may be his feeling that "facts" are neither primary nor solid, but the phenomena of a dream. So pervasive is dream or reverie in Longfellow's imagination that his most effective lyric or meditative poems are likely to be built on dreamlike associations, and the felicitous "legend style," as he called it, of some of his longer works depends upon an atmosphere of dreamy distance.

When physical surfaces lose their bounds and firmness, the natural world is easily invaded by the circumambient world of spirit. From the early "Footsteps of Angels" to the late "Helen of Tyre," Longfellow's poetry is recurrently haunted by phantoms, as the planes of nature and spirit, always thought by Longfellow to be exactly correspondent, seem to converge at a visionary point somewhere between reality and unreality. Longfellow's belief in the interaction of the invisible world and the world of sense led him actually to experiment with spiritualism a few times. In practice, he found spiritualism unconvincing and unedifying, but he never lost the sense of continuity between this world and another, between the living and the dead, that makes the pervasive mysteriousness of many poems so memorable.

To withdraw into the haunted night, to surrender to nostalgia and reverie, was Longfellow's natural inclination, intensified by his domestic catastrophes and, in his later years, by loneliness. His beliefs and character, however, prohibited such a retreat: the voices of night must be answered by the voices of day, or by aspiration the dreaming night must be made holy with stars. To assert present reality and the possibility of meaningful action in it becomes the necessary countermovement against the pull of the past; it is the thrust of health against incipient morbidity. On the side of reality are religious faith, human love, and the achievements and obligations of civilization; these are the foundations of hope and inescapable duty. Thus the longing for imaginative flight is characteristically confronted by a resolute will: this was the fundamental conflict in Longfellow's experience and, mirrored in his art, provides the only continuous tension in a poetry whose structure and language have little of that quality.

The conflict is often described rather than presented, and the resolution stated rather than achieved. Even in such simple poems, however, there is occasionally a conviction successfully communicated that seems unaccountably to be an increment from the underlying experience itself. In the once over-acclaimed, now over-abused "A Psalm of Life," the conflict exists chiefly as a background for the celebration of triumphant resolve, directly expressed. That this hortatory poem should have a witnessed effect denied to countless other exhortations may be due to a residual force not earned, according to the modern prescription, through the strategy of the poem itself, but subtly transmitted to it as a tone from the prior struggle and its resolution that was indeed earned, since "A Psalm of Life" springs from the same experience that produced *Hyperion*. In Longfellow's more complex didactic poems

24

the countering assertion of hope or purpose is not always poetically successful; at times it is imposed, or inadequate to the strength of the preceding melancholy. But in the best poems it is sufficiently implied in the foregoing situation or images to be a valid climax.

The major ideas of Longfellow are clearly reflected in his poetry considered as a whole; he repeatedly makes explicit reference to them, and indulges in overt teaching based upon them. His poetry, nevertheless, is not a poetry of ideas: certainly it is not philosophic or genuinely reflective, if "reflective" implies extended analysis of experience and systematic deliberation upon it. Except occasionally and on some few subjects, notably art, Longfellow's poems are primarily meditative; they express intuitions of experience, whether personal or literary, their thought usually arising immediately from feeling and remaining closely attached to it, or interwoven with it. Habitually, there is little progressive development of idea or attitude: a poem's underlying experience is made concrete in a described object, situation, or story — an image whose significance is presented sometimes as almost a short allegorization, more often as a correspondence or connotation on another plane. Since the image, from whatever source it is drawn and however simple or complex it may be, not only determines the tone of the whole poem but is also the essential figure of the experience, Longfellow's meditative poetry is, on the whole, fundamentally metaphoric, although in many poems the lack of compression, the extended statement, and the failure to renew conventional images all dissipate metaphor's possible intensity.

Some of Longfellow's important images by their complexity, recurrence, and stability become true symbols, at times restricted or extensively modified by particular contexts, but possessing a sufficiently persistent significance throughout the poetry to express Longfellow's imaginative apprehension of life. A few symbols are based on artifacts or on artistic creation — bells, walled forts or castles, music — but most are drawn from nature. Largely traditional, they are sometimes casually used as cultural hand-me-downs; more often, however, their significance has clearly been rediscovered at a deep level of experience. The most pervasive symbols are archetypal: the darkness of haunted night, oblivion, and the past, whose chill is the coldness of the grave; the warm light of reality, of vital energy, and, for Longfellow, of love, concentrated in the sun; water, whose flow is the motion of feeling, spirit, and time, and whose fluidity Longfellow attributes also to sky, air, and light; the stars of divine or spiritual order and, more personally, of aspiration.

Above all others are the symbols drawn from Longfellow's memory of youthful experience; his landscape of the human situation and of individual inner life is that of the Maine coastline: the sea, the nearby forest, and the narrow habitable strip between. This last, the scene of rational and civilized life, additionally provides a symbol of precarious security, the home centered in the hearth, whose warmth is the focus of human relationships and a protection against the storms without: although Longfellow's fireside scene is likely to be sentimentalized, it occasionally reflects in muted fashion the ancient image of man huddled by his saving fire. The forest, boundless and majestic, frequently wailing in the wind, embodies a primitive life somewhat ominous for civilized man. The sea is Longfellow's deepest and most inclusive symbol; no contemporary writer save Melville was more profoundly or constantly responsive to it. In Longfellow's poetry, the sea is the restless mystery of existence, and its unfathomable source; it is the energy of unconfined and subconscious life, and of liberty. In its effects, it is also paradoxical, merciful and merciless, purifying yet dangerous, at once death-giving and life-giving.

In spite of the importance of images and symbols, however, the typical movement of a poem by Longfellow is toward a formulated decision; that is, however complex the underlying feelings or situation, any tension or conflict, or any balance of opposites, is resolved by a choice amongst the possibilities or by a limiting statement of specific significance. Since the poems ordinarily do not fully present whatever struggle or turbulence there may have been in the originating experience, but only selected, usually subdued aspects of it, the resolution often appears easy or oversimplified. In the best poems, however, the concluding statement is at once a natural consequence of an imaginative prior development and an explication sufficiently complex to embrace all the possibilities.

The lyric and meditative poems, and several of the shorter narratives, are characteristically, although not exclusively, developed in distinguishable stages, moving from image to analogy or statement, or from image to analogy to statement; much more rarely, from statement to image. In a large number of the poems, the image is fully presented in one or more initial stanzas or verse paragraphs and its moral or spiritual significance set forth in the following ones, frequently with an exact correspondence in the lengths of presentation and of statement, a balance well exemplified in "Seaweed" and "The Beleaguered City." Alternatively, the statement may be a comparatively brief conclusion, or even a counterstatement of denial, revulsion, or change of direction, as in "The Bells of San Blas," rather than a climax to what has preceded it. In many poems, the movement between image and comparison or statement is continuously back and forth, the image being presented in steps, each of which is accompanied by an immediate reflection upon it. The poems that do not move by clearly defined stages may conveniently be designated as one-stage. Classification by stages, however, can be only approximate: an indicated spiritual significance, for example, may cling so closely to an image, as it does in "Sandalphon," that it seems simply to be an overtone of it.

In the one-stage poems, the presentation may be hortatory, descriptive, or narrative; it either produces a direct, uncomplicated, often emotional effect or clearly implies a further meaning without openly indicating or stating it. Into this category fall most of the short narratives and also many of the poems most appealing to modern taste, the quasi-imagistic poems that present a concentrated image with expanding overtones: "Chrysaor," "The Bells of Lynn," "Aftermath," "The Tide Rises, the Tide Falls" are representative of this group, and "The Ropewalk" is similar in its reliance on suggestion, although it employs a series of images, central and associated, rather than one image alone. A few two-stage poems are also primarily imagistic in effect, some of them, like "The Warning," developing their analogy closely in terms of the original image, others, like "Snowflakes," using their analogy actually to reinforce the image. However stimulating Longfellow's imagistic poems may be, they are nonetheless too small in number to be typical of his poetry.

The three-stage poems usually consist of initial image, analogy, and explicit statement, with attention more or less evenly distributed among them, a method that is obvious in the three stanzas of the feeble "Rainy Day," whose initial lines run "The day is cold, and dark, and dreary . . . My life is cold, and dark, and dreary . . . Be still, sad heart! and cease repining . . ." For some reason, the three-stage poems include many of Longfellow's bad and indifferent pieces; on the other hand, they also include some of the more completely satisfying meditative verses, such as "Palingenesis" and a sensitively wrought ode, "The Building of the Ship," whose oratorically eloquent, hortatory last stanza begins with the familiar "Thou, too, sail on, O Ship of State!" and makes an illogical but emotionally appropriate and powerful new appli-

cation of the poem's structural analogy between the construction
and launching of a ship and the progress of romantic love cli-
maxed in marriage.

The largest number of Longfellow's shorter poems, including
the sonnets and such important compositions as the brief "In the
Churchyard at Cambridge" and "Jugurtha" and the lengthier
"Fire of Driftwood," "My Lost Youth," and "Morituri Salutamus,"
are two-stage; if his imagination found any method especially congenial, it is this one, so that his notable achievement in sonnet
form is not surprising.

The early two- or three-stage poems usually end in explicit decla-
ration; after the mid-1840's there is increasing reliance on a final
metaphor or symbol, as in "Autumn Within":

> It is autumn; not without,
>   But within me is the cold.
> Youth and spring are all about;
>   It is I that have grown old.
>
> Birds are darting through the air,
>   Singing, building without rest;
> Life is stirring everywhere,
>   Save within my lonely breast.
>
> There is silence: the dead leaves
>   Fall and rustle and are still;
> Beats no flail upon the sheaves,
>   Comes no murmur from the mill.

The poem is too short to be widely representative, but it bears the
Longfellow impress: the quatrains observe a 2-2 rhetorical division; the lines are four-stress, in falling rhythm; the accommoda-
tions of stress and pause to meaning are minor but careful; the
language is simple and the word order nearly normal, save for
the deliberate departure in the concluding lines; there is a touch
of showy pathos in the eighth line; the images are traditional,

and, especially in the last two lines, rather "poetic" or literary. The fundamental comparison of inner states and outer seasons allows easy further comparison between seasons and thus inner states, and so moves into the suggestive final revelation of age's fruitlessness in a favorite image: the cessation of sound. In so short a poem, the procedure is abbreviated but clear. The initial image is quickly introduced in three words; its spiritual significance is explicitly stated at once; the comparison is somewhat tenuously explored, and the conclusion intensifies the comparison by shifting the images associated with autumn to the signified spiritual state. Like so many of Longfellow's good if obviously minor poems, this has a personal feeling that manages, even if barely, to come through the conventional scenery; it also has something of Longfellow's typical facility, attended, as often, by the bad and good angels of glibness and grace.

Like much nineteenth-century poetry, Longfellow's seems in retrospect leisurely, even too relaxed. The slow development of ideas, the elaboration of details, the multiplication of parallels, the explication of the already-evident are practices that destroy some of his poems and in varying combinations and degrees characterize most of them. The language, too, bears the stamp of its time in its tendency to expansive statement, its often predictable vocabulary and phraseology, and its fondness for literary diction. Like the sporadic addiction to poetically picturesque subject matter, these qualities are alien to sophisticated modern taste, although whether or to what extent they are necessarily faults is a problem of literary theory and the absoluteness of critical standards. Historically considered, the kind of poetry Longfellow wrote lay within a poetic tradition that with various adaptations served the larger part of a century, and was imaginatively satisfying to the romantic-Victorian sensibility. Within the age's literary conventions, Longfellow used language skillfully and sensitively. At its best, his language is simple and economical, natural in movement, emotionally exact in its use of words and phrases, and restrained in statement. Furthermore, Longfellow's handling of language is largely responsible for his achievement of an impressive tonal range from the formality of semi-epic narrative to the humor-seasoned easiness of the discourse of polite society. He makes the traditional poetic language, with often minimal alteration, express distinctively his own insights and feelings.

As a poet more evocative than creative of experience, Longfellow employs language with a notable awareness of the way in which it becomes charged with meaning from the inescapable situations of human life. Frequently he depends not upon connotations or overtones developed within the context of a poem, but upon a resonance provided immediately by general experience itself and renewed in the poem by allusions to the appropriate common events or situations, or by brief descriptions of them. This habit demands from the reader a supply of significance from his private store and a willingness to accept suggestive reference rather than precise control in the poem — a concession not demanded by great poetry, and by some critics austerely refused to any. It is, however, a concession habitually made to occasional poems, whose otherwise vague or flabby language may acquire exactness from setting and event. When, in "Morituri Salutamus," Longfellow recalls his audience from thoughts of friends dead and buried to

> . . . these scenes frequented by our feet
> When we were young, and life was fresh and sweet,

the last line is not vaguely sentimental, but, like the poem's title, genuinely moving because emotionally appropriate and provided with definable meaning by the situation: an aging poet addressing the dwindled number of college classmates at certainly their last reunion, held fifty years after graduation.

Like other aspects of his poetry, Longfellow's prosody is remarkable for resourcefulness and variety within traditional limits. His uncommon talent in versification and his absorption in its technical problems led to no prosodic revolution; indeed, a dangerous facility, combined with a taste for euphony, brings his verse at moments close to that of the typical Victorian "sweet singer." Within accepted bounds, however, Longfellow's versatility in rhythmical, metrical, and rhyming patterns and his constant experimentation, directed toward the creation of a unique effect for each poem, reveal a technical mastery rarely approached in American poetry. Although his prosodic variety is most obvious in the surprisingly various patterns of his stanzaic verse, it is perhaps more subtly displayed in meeting the resistance of a set form like the sonnet, where, employing the Italian pattern and almost invariably observing a strict octet-sestet division, Longfellow achieves striking rhythmic differences by ingenious handling of metrical substitution, run-on and end-stopped lines, and caesuras. In freer forms, his skill is no less evident: the extremely uneven blank verse of *The Divine Tragedy* has reflective passages in which comparative rhythmic freedom works with approximately normal word order to produce lines that sometimes collapse into prose but that occasionally attain a thoroughly natural movement barely but unmistakably tightened into poetry, as in the course of the soliloquy by Manahem the Essenian in the third part of the "First Passover":

> The things that have been and shall be no more,
> The things that are, and that hereafter shall be,
> The things that might have been, and yet were not,
> The fading twilight of great joys departed,
> The daybreak of great truths as yet unrisen,
> The intuition and the expectation
> Of something, which, when come, is not the same,
> But only like its forecast in men's dreams,

> The longing, the delay, and the delight,
> Sweeter for the delay; youth, hope, love, death,
> And disappointment which is also death,
> All these make up the sum of human life;
> A dream within a dream, a wind at night
> Howling across the desert in despair,
> Seeking for something lost it cannot find.

The technical virtuosity of Longfellow's art is manifested in several accomplishments: the successful maintenance of falling rhythm in spite of English poetry's strong tendency to rising rhythm; the dexterous control of varied rhythm and free rhyming by an organization based on parallelism, balance, and alliteration; and the giving of widely varied movement to such uncomplicated verse forms as the quatrain. Even so straightforward a narrative as "Paul Revere" shows a meticulous attention to technical detail that partly accounts for the rather complex effect of an apparently simple poem. As a rule, the closer the examination of Longfellow's verse technique, the greater is the appreciation of a diversity that can succeed in the subdued four-line stanzas of his meditative poetry, the stately hexameters of *Evangeline*, and the jaunty tetrameter couplets of "The Rhyme of Sir Christopher."

The shorter poems of Longfellow enjoyed a contemporary popularity, in England and other countries as well as in America, that has rarely been rivaled, yet it was not these poems but his long ones on which his reputation chiefly rested, especially the long narratives: *Evangeline, Hiawatha, The Courtship of Miles Standish,* and *Tales of a Wayside Inn.* More recently the major narrative poems have been relegated to the classroom, often at a rather elementary level, in acknowledgment of Longfellow's ability to tell a story in them, and with the implication that he does no more. The nineteenth century knew better: when *Evangeline* was published in 1847, one English reviewer hailed it as "the first genuine Castalian fount which has burst from the soil of America!"

In spite of his fanciful image, the critic was properly celebrating what was in fact the first important sustained poem by an American and was endorsing the general acclaim that made *Evangeline* herself a symbol of the Acadian "cause."

Like all of Longfellow's major poems, *Evangeline* was, in modern academic jargon, "well researched," and one result of Longfellow's reading was to make the poem in part a richly descriptive tour of expanses of western and southern America. The story itself, however, is an altogether simple one, whose essentials were first given to Longfellow by Hawthorne: in the dispersal of the French Acadians in 1755, two lovers, Evangeline and Gabriel, are separated, and for weary years Evangeline attempts to trace Gabriel through the settlements and wilds of the American colonies; finally, aging and losing earthly hope, she becomes a Sister of Mercy in a Philadelphia hospital, where, during a plague, the dying Gabriel is brought and the lovers are reunited just before his death. Gabriel early recedes into the background as the sought rather than seeker, and the focus of the whole poem is upon Evangeline, giving the temperamentally chivalric Longfellow full scope for the development of an idealized, simple woman of absolute fidelity, the kind of heroine most congenial to his imagination. In a realistically represented milieu Evangeline would seem too etherealized but the deliberately legendary treatment of the story and the touch of dreamlike remoteness in the setting create an idyllic effect appropriate to the characterization. Moreover, the idealization of the heroine is closely related to the poem's meaning: Evangeline is increasingly spiritualized by the patiently endured sufferings of her nearly endless journey until she finally emerges as a saintly figure.

The journey of Evangeline and the whole story in which she moves are raised to semiheroic proportions by Longfellow's mythologizing of his materials. Acadia is also Arcadia; the simple lives of the peasants, viewed under a summer sun, recall the Golden Age and Eden, and the murmuring pines and hemlocks color the scene with childhood innocence recalled. With expulsion and separation, a mythic pattern specifically Christian develops: the pious Evangeline is the exiled wayfarer making her dedicated journey through the world to her final renunciation of it and her entering upon the more purely spiritual pilgrimage of return to the true Arcadia of Heaven, where alone reunion can be lasting. When the two lovers at one dramatic point miss each other by the narrowest of margins, it is, as one critic has said, like the touch of God's hand reserving Evangeline for another marriage. Despite the slowness and occasional thinness of the narration, the pattern of *Evangeline* gives the poem substance and dignity.

In creating the hexameter lines of *Evangeline* Longfellow sensibly treated the problem of English hexameter as a practical one, and paid little heed to the theoretic objections that have enlivened criticism since the Renaissance. Encouraged by Goethe's example and by the experiments of Southey and Coleridge, he solved the immediate problems by using a basically dactyllic line with a trochaic close and free trochaic substitution; the minimally necessary spondees he obtained by juxtaposing monosyllabic words and by coaxing the second syllable of trochees into an approximation of spondees. The resultant hexameters give *Evangeline* a slow processional movement; the longer line admits lavish introduction of concrete detail through additional modifying words, and has a pleasantly lingering effect appropriate to idyllic tone, as Longfellow apparently realized, since extended use of hexameters occurs chiefly in his idylls — *Evangeline, The Courtship of Miles Standish,* and "Elizabeth" in *Tales of a Wayside Inn.*

The Courtship of Miles Standish, although published eleven years later, resembles *Evangeline* in measure, in use of a legendary-historical foundation, and in pastoral coloring. The *Courtship*, however, has a vein of humor that leaves readers suspended between sentiment and amusement. The story has long since passed into folklore: how John Alden loved Priscilla Mullins but, out of friendship, wooed her in Captain Miles Standish's behalf, and how, with a false report of Standish's death, John and Priscilla married, with the captain returning just in time to assent. It is not the tale but the telling that has distinction. Longfellow moves through variations of tone with impressive assurance, from satirical humor to romance tinged with sentimentality, through sobriety and comedy alternatively.

The success of the *Courtship* lies principally in its humorous juxtaposition of two extravagant attitudes, each described in appropriate language and imagery, with each other and with common sense. One attitude is embodied in Captain Miles Standish, the hot-tempered commander of a twelve-man army, a swaggerer, a valiant man, and a student of the wars of the Hebrews, Caesar's *Commentaries*, and an artillery guide "designed for belligerent Christians"; on the other side is John Alden, sincere, hard-working, over-scrupulous, compelled to disguise pleasure as duty before he can enjoy it, and fearful lest his preference of love over friendship may be "worshipping Astaroth blindly, and impious idols of Baal." At the center is common-sensical Priscilla, quiet, loving, amused at her suitors' posturings, and busy at the spinning wheel emblematic of settled life with its civilizing domesticity.

The marriage of John and Priscilla, however humorous its preliminaries, is nevertheless, in the barely surviving Plymouth colony that is the setting, an affirmation of faith in America's future and a promise of its fruitfulness. Thus the almost lush description of the climactic bridal day is without serious incongruity set forth in images of religious ritual and of fertility, as the sun issues forth like a high priest, with the sea a laver at his feet, and

Priscilla rides on a snow-white bull to her wedding while golden sunlight gleams on bunches of purple grapes. Longfellow again introduces the imagery of Eden and expulsion as he describes the land of privation and hardship lying before John and Priscilla, and adds,

> But to their eyes transfigured, it seemed as the Garden
> of Eden,
> Filled with the presence of God, whose voice was the
> sound of the ocean.

The final balance of sometimes broad humor, romantic sentiment, and gravity is a tonal achievement of no small order.

With *Hiawatha* Longfellow made his chief contribution to nineteenth-century American literature's search for a usable national past, whose necessity to the creation of a native culture was assumed from the analogy of European cultural history. America's antiquity, however, was Indian and primitively tribal, and therefore both racially and culturally alien. The pieties of nationalism nonetheless demanded that the gap between the two worlds be bridged; countless authors valiantly responded, and, with a few notable exceptions, artistically perished in the attempt. To Longfellow the whole effort seemed misdirected, since America's cultural past was essentially European, although he had been long interested in Indian lore and history, and was acquainted with such authorities on Indian life as Heckewelder and Schoolcraft. Typically, he found his own formula for relating the Indian past to the American present in a European national poem, the Finnish *Kalevala*, which suggested the use of legends linked together by the central figure of a culture hero, the creations of myth and folklore being, for the cultivated imagination, more viable than the grubby data of actual primitive living. In American terms, the Indians' passage from savagery to a low level of civilization could be treated as preparatory to the climactic arrival of high civilization represented by the white man, and poetry could thus create the continuity that history had failed to provide. One result of this plan is the weakest moment in *Hiawatha*, when the hero unreservedly recommends to his people the religion and culture of the white man, represented by the Jesuit missionaries: the abrupt transition from a legendary world to that of fictionalized history is unconvincing, as it was probably certain to be, in spite of its theoretical justification as a means of relating Indian and white civilization, the chief desideratum of the age.

Like the creators of the Noble Redman, Longfellow adapted his Indians to contemporary tastes and interests. His hero is a bowdlerized version of a mythic Algonkian chief, and Hiawatha's romance with Minnehaha is conducted by the rules of sentimental fiction. The idealization, however, is largely intended by Longfellow, as a part of the deliberately legendary atmosphere of the narration. Criticisms based on realistic assumptions, whether Emerson's mild blame or Schoolcraft's praise, were, in Longfellow's eyes, fundamentally irrelevant: Hiawatha was, he stated, a kind of "American Prometheus," and the poem was "an Indian Edda," a recognizably poetic romance, based on ancient myths and traditions and thus to be read as an attractively colorful reflection not of Indian actuality, but of primitive imagination.

The language and versification of *Hiawatha* were designed as part of its legendary effect. The trochaic tetrameter meter, suggested by the *Kalevala* and by earlier Indian romances, has an accentuation sufficiently strong to invite easy exaggeration into singsong, an invitation readily accepted by most modern readers. In so long a poem, the conspicuous rhythm, the constant use of parallelism and repetition, the profusion of exotic Indian names, and the simple personifications all finally threaten monotony and make parody irresistible. Critical objections to *Hiawatha*'s verse can be countered only by treating the verse, according to Longfellow's intention, as a part of the primitive machinery. Thus regarded, the verse loses its apparent eccentricity and contributes a suitable effect of chant and of quaintness to the legendary atmosphere Longfellow sought to create. Unfortunately, it also heightens the sense of artifice pervasive in *Hiawatha* and perhaps inseparable from a pseudo-primitive genre.

Present-day concern with myth, legend, and folklore gives *Hiawatha* a more serious interest than it possessed in the recent past, even if the modern reader usually prefers to take his myth neat or as revitalized in current forms. The episodes of *Hiawatha* are based upon now familiar mythic patterns. Hiawatha himself, begotten by the West Wind upon the daughter of moon-descended Nokomis, is a demigod aligning himself with humanity. He teaches his people how to plant and cultivate maize, and begins to instruct them in the arts of civilization, the skills of fishing and agriculture, and the art of picture-writing. With the help of his few close companions and of the helpful animals of folklore, he slays the spirit of evil, the serpent-guarded Magician, and Pau-Puk-Keewis, the champion of the old, anarchic savagery, and finally departs for the Islands of the Blessed. From one standpoint, *Hiawatha* is a set of picturesque variations on mythic themes, and its recapitulation of a whole mythic pattern gives it in its entirety an imaginative strength greater than its incidental faults would apparently support. Its major weakness as a whole arises primarily from its literarily calculated primitivism: the sophistication of its simplicity makes it too manifestly a tour de force.

Longfellow's last major narrative work, *Tales of a Wayside Inn*, was published in three installments over an eleven-year period. The design of the work, a collection of stories in a unifying framework, recalls the *Canterbury Tales*, but Longfellow's self-confessed inability to rival Chaucer makes the Chaucerian work properly a point of reference rather than of comparison. In Longfellow's

Tales, the stories are clearly primary, the framework a support. The setting is the Red Lion Inn (now the reconstructed Wayside Inn) in Sudbury, Massachusetts, a hostelry well known to Longfellow and his friends. The narrators, designated by profession, avocation, nationality, or race, are all based upon actual acquaintances of Longfellow's: the Poet was Theophilus Parsons, a translator of Dante; the Musician was the Norwegian violinist Ole Bull; the Sicilian was Luigi Monti, an instructor in Harvard's modern languages department. Their individual characteristics are generalized into more or less typical ones, but there can be no satirical representation or socially or dramatically significant quarreling: the narrators form a friendly and homogeneous group. What is possible is realized — an animated running discussion of topics suggested by the tales and of points of view expressed by the tellers. In flexible tetrameter couplets, Longfellow takes the discussion from aesthetics to religion, and achieves an effect of individually colored discourse sufficient to support the tales and often interesting in itself.

Individually considered, the tales vary greatly in nature, interest, and quality. A few, like "Lady Wentworth" and "Azrael," dwindle into anecdote, and others, like "The Ballad of Carmilhan," are principally evocative of mood or of that ghostly atmosphere that Longfellow could always effectively create. Most of the stories, however, are marked by Longfellow's real narrative talent: the ability to make well-selected, continuously progressing events and vividly, if broadly, drawn characters deliver in a climactic scene some comment upon an aspect of life or a typical movement of human feeling. The accomplishment of the *Tales,* however, lies less in particular stories, as good as several of them are, than in the variety of the gathered narratives. Contrasting with each other in scene, tone, and poetic structure, and held together by the framework, the stories in juxtaposition suggest the

40

inclusive range possible to the simple, immemorial activity of storytelling, and the way in which even traditional tales may reflect attitudes and feelings of the narrators. Many kinds of effects are embraced, from the grimness of "Torquemada" to the broad fabliau humor of "The Monk of Casal-Maggiore" or the vividness of "The Saga of King Olaf," one of the most vigorous of all Longfellow's poems, with its balladlike but well-developed dramatization of the mingled zeal and barbarism of the first Viking champions and enemies of Christianity. Moreover, a few of the tales, like "Emma and Eginhard" and "The Falcon of Ser Federigo," reflect a more realistic and tolerant assessment of human behavior than Longfellow's poetry commonly displays. The reputation of the *Tales* is unavoidably linked to the fortunes of narrative poetry, especially of straightforward narrative; within that limited area, the *Tales* occupies a place of considerable honor.

The major irony of Longfellow's literary career was the commitment of his hopes for distinctive major achievement to the form in which he was most consistently unsuccessful, the poetic drama. From 1849 to 1872 he intermittently labored over what he regarded as "his loftier song" in "sublimer strain," as his greatest work, "the equivalent expression for the trouble and wrath of life, for its sorrow and mystery." The completed *Christus: A Mystery* consists of three parts comprising four poetic dramas, all so manifestly closet dramas that they could be properly described as dramatically organized poems. The first part is *The Divine Tragedy*, the last to be published; the second part is *The Golden Legend*, the first published; the third part, *The New England Tragedies*, consists of two dramas, *John Endicott* and *Giles Corey of the Salem Farms*. The three parts are linked by interludes and the whole *Christus* is provided with an "Introitus" and "Finale." No other works of Longfellow's had such intended scope or received such dedicated attention; and none were so disappointing in result. The twenty-odd years spent in composition, the lapse of time between publication of the parts, and the fact that each part is also a substantially self-contained work explain why the *Christus* seems partly to be an assemblage; indeed, it is surprising that the whole does achieve a loose unity which makes it more than the sum of its parts.

Longfellow's general failure in dramatic form is understandable. His talent was narrative and lyrically meditative, and he could not refrain from reliance on narration and exposition, even to the destruction of dramatic effect. The sequence and relationship of episodes and actions is basically determined, especially in the last two parts of the *Christus*, by narrative not dramatic logic and development. It is thus unfortunate that from 1849 on he increasingly looked to drama as the vehicle of his most important ideas. It is his least pretentious dramatic work, the early *Spanish Student*, that is in many respects the most successfully realized; in spite of its lack of intellectual significance, it is a colorful, pleasant comedy of intrigue, technically more proficient than the later poetic dramas. Two minor dramatic works, *Judas Maccabeus* and *The Masque of Pandora*, have interesting themes but are extremely weak in execution. Only the partly completed *Michael Angelo*, closely related to Longfellow's own life and work, and containing in a few passages some of his strongest poetry, shows an apparently emerging mastery of dramatic form in the 1870's.

The fundamental obstacle to the *Christus'* success, however, is not simply a flawed dramatic technique, but an internal conflict in the work between its ostensible intention and its meaning. Originally planned as a dramatizing of the progress of Christianity, the *Christus* loosely employs the theological virtues of faith, hope, and charity as the basis of organization, *The Divine Tragedy* expressing hope through its representation of Christ's life and mission, the *Golden Legend* depicting faith in its full medieval flowering, and the *New England Tragedies* pointing to the religious freedom of the age of charity or love. The optimism of the design is realized in some scenes and is recurrently asserted as a proposition, but it is not borne out in the *Christus'* development and accumulated feeling, which are finally somber and even pessimistic in their tendency. Longfellow's emotional recoil from several aspects of the contemporary religious scene apparently caused him to lose much of his professed hope for the future and left its mark especially on the first and third parts, the latest composed, of the *Christus*. If the last part inculcates love and tolerance at all, it does so only by exhibiting the horrors of bigotry, and the relentless power of intolerance is in fact the dominant force; in *John Endicott* a series of special providences, occurring near the conclusion, indicate divine displeasure with persecution, but the Quakers are saved only by an intervening royal mandate of that unlikely *deus ex machina*, Charles II; in the final, still grimmer *Giles Corey*, where the maliciously accused though innocent Corey is put to death by pressing, this climactic scene is followed by a hasty, excessively short speech by Cotton Mather predicting that never again will such things happen, a judgment perhaps validated by history, but certainly not by the action or tone of the drama. Furthermore, the interlude preparing for the *New England Tragedies* is a soliloquy by Martin Luther that alternates between an announcement of spiritual freedom recovered from religious tyranny and a condemnation of humanism reflecting the sectarianism and hatred most repellent to Longfellow: it is an unpromising introduction to the latest stage of an assertedly progressive historical movement.

That the *New England Tragedies* made a darkened climax Longfellow was probably aware. He originally planned a third, more confident concluding play based on the simple, pious life of Pennsylvania's Moravian sisterhood. This, however, he never wrote, and its abandonment may be explained by the actual state of his sentiments and the developing mood of the *Christus*. In the *Divine Tragedy*, the part latest in composition, Longfellow examines that most persistent and personal of his themes, the problem of dream and reality. The fear expressed throughout is that all life is a delusive dream within a dream, and Christus the visionary of an unreal kingdom. The act of faith thus becomes primarily an assertion of reality, its validity being finally confirmed by the appearance of the risen Christus. Yet the haunting fear is too powerfully expressed to be dispelled even by an apparently victorious conclusion.

The "Introitus" opening the *Christus* finds in the sadness of pre-Christian ages the signs of a coming Redeemer. The "Finale," however, is not a celebration of redemption achieved, but a melancholy review of the Christian centuries, insisting that "the evil doth not cease." The survey is not despairing, but its limited hope is proclaimed in spite of rather than out of Christian history, and hope's realization seems indefinitely postponed:

> Poor, sad Humanity
> Through all the dust and heat
> Turns back with bleeding feet,
> By the weary road it came . . .

So the tracing of the human condition comes nearly full circle back to the "Introitus," and is saved from cyclical completion only by Longfellow's characteristic emphasis upon the persistence of the ideal and the possibility of individual Christian action.

The study of Longfellow's poetic reputation is perhaps more relevant to the history of criticism than to the evaluation of his art. His most literate contemporaries delivered varying decisions, some finding the poetry seriously deficient, others praising it without reservation, most setting a very high value on the best poems while pointing out the weakness of others. It was popular acclaim, hailing the man as much as the poet, that elevated Longfellow to a position no sober critical judgment could sanction. With the emergence of modern literature and the literary wars it evoked, the defenders of the new order found it necessary and not unpleasant to counter the hostility of presumably Victorian attitudes by attacking Victorian ideals and achievements. In America, Longfellow, in his popular canonization, offered himself as the surest target for an assault on the nineteenth century; at the nadir, one influential critic advanced the proposition that Longfellow's poetry has no iota of the poetic character. Later, however, as the early twentieth-century revolution itself receded into the past, it became possible for Longfellow to share in the general revaluation of Victorian literature. To this more objective examination, dating especially from Odell Shepard's reserved but often acute essay prefixed to his selective edition of Longfellow's poems, many studies have contributed, including such recent full-length ones as Lawrance Thompson's reassessment of the young Longfellow's experience, Edward Wagenknecht's important and sympathetic interpretation of Longfellow as person and author, and Newton Arvin's uniquely valuable analysis of the poetry as a whole. From this continuing reconsideration has come a clear view of the many limitations of Longfellow's talent, but also a new respect for his accomplishment within them.

✒ Selected Bibliography

Principal Works of Henry Wadsworth Longfellow

Coplas de Don Jorge Manrique, Translated from the Spanish . . . Boston: Allen and Ticknor, 1833.

Outre-Mer: A Pilgrimage beyond the Sea. 2 vols. Boston: Hilliard, Gray (Vol. I), Lilly, Wait (Vol. II), 1833–34.

Hyperion: A Romance. 2 vols. New York: S. Colman, 1839.

Voices of the Night. Cambridge, Mass.: J. Owen, 1839.

Ballads and Other Poems. Cambridge, Mass.: J. Owen, 1841.

Poems on Slavery. Cambridge, Mass.: J. Owen, 1842.

The Spanish Student, A Play in Three Acts. Cambridge, Mass.: J. Owen, 1843.

The Poets and Poetry of Europe, with Introductions and Biographical Notices by Henry Wadsworth Longfellow. Philadelphia: Carey and Hart, 1845.

The Belfry of Bruges and Other Poems. Cambridge, Mass.: J. Owen, 1846.

Evangeline, a Tale of Acadie. Boston: Ticknor, 1847.

Kavanagh, a Tale. Boston: Ticknor, Reed, and Fields, 1849.

The Seaside and the Fireside. Boston: Ticknor, Reed, and Fields, 1850.

The Golden Legend. Boston: Ticknor, Reed, and Fields, 1851.

The Song of Hiawatha. Boston: Ticknor and Fields, 1855.

Drift Wood, A Collection of Essays. Boston: Ticknor and Fields, 1857.

The Courtship of Miles Standish and Other Poems. Boston: Ticknor and Fields, 1858.

Tales of a Wayside Inn. Boston: Ticknor and Fields, 1863.

The Divine Comedy of Dante Alighieri, Translated by Henry Wadsworth Longfellow. 3 vols. Boston: Ticknor and Fields, 1865–67.

Flower-de-Luce. Boston: Ticknor and Fields, 1867.

The New England Tragedies. Boston: Ticknor and Fields, 1868. (Privately printed, 1867.)

The Divine Tragedy. Boston: Osgood, 1871.

Christus: A Mystery. 3 vols. Boston: Osgood, 1872.

Three Books of Song. Boston: Osgood, 1872.

Aftermath. Boston: Osgood, 1873.

The Hanging of the Crane. Boston: Mifflin, 1874.

The Masque of Pandora and Other Poems. Boston: Osgood, 1875.

Kéramos and Other Poems. Boston: Houghton, Osgood, 1878.

Ultima Thule. Boston: Mifflin, 1880.
In the Harbor. Boston: Houghton, Mifflin, 1882.
Michael Angelo. London: Houghton, Mifflin, 1883.

Selected and Collected Editions

Complete Works, edited by Horace E. Scudder. Riverside Edition. 11 vols. Boston: Houghton, Mifflin, 1886. Reprinted in Standard Library Edition, with *Life* by Samuel Longfellow and illustrations. 14 vols. Boston: Houghton, Mifflin, 1891. Reprinted also in Craigie Edition, with illustrations. 11 vols. Boston: Houghton, Mifflin, 1904.

Complete Poetical Works, edited by Horace E. Scudder. Cambridge Edition. Boston: Houghton, Mifflin, 1893. Reprinted in Household Edition, with illustrations. Boston: Houghton, Mifflin, 1902.

Longfellow's Boyhood Poems, edited by George T. Little. Saratoga Springs, N.Y.: Ray W. Pettengill, 1925.

Henry Wadsworth Longfellow: Representative Selections, with introduction, bibliography, and notes by Odell Shepard. American Writers Series. New York: American Book, 1934.

Current American Reprints

Longfellow: Selected Poetry, with an introduction by Howard Nemerov. Laurel Poetry Series. New York: Dell. $.35.

Dante's Inferno, Translated by Henry Wadsworth Longfellow; revised and edited with a new introduction by Bernard Stambler. New York: Collier Books. $.95.

Bibliographies

Dana, H. W. L. "Henry Wadsworth Longfellow," in Vol. II of the *Cambridge History of American Literature.* 4 vols. New York: G. P. Putnam's Sons, 1917.

Livingston, Luther S. *A Bibliography of the First Editions in Book Form of the Writings of Henry Wadsworth Longfellow.* New York: Privately printed, 1908.

Critical and Biographical Studies

Arms, George T. "Longfellow," in *The Fields Were Green.* Stanford, Calif.: Stanford University Press, 1948.

Arvin, Newton. *Longfellow: His Life and Work.* Boston: Little, Brown, 1963.

Austin, George L. *Henry Wadsworth Longfellow: His Life, His Works, His Friendships.* Boston: Lee and Shepard, 1883.

47

Gorman, Herbert. *A Victorian American, Henry Wadsworth Longfellow.* New York: Doran, 1926.

Hatfield, James T. *New Light on Longfellow, with Special Reference to His Relations with Germany.* Boston: Houghton, Mifflin, 1933.

Hawthorne, Manning, and Henry Dana. *The Origin and Development of Longfellow's "Evangeline."* Portland, Maine: Anthoensen Press, 1947.

Higginson, Thomas W. *Henry Wadsworth Longfellow.* American Men of Letters Series. Boston: Houghton, Mifflin, 1902.

Hilen, Andrew. *Longfellow and Scandinavia.* New Haven, Conn.: Yale University Press, 1947.

Johnson, Carl L. *Professor Longfellow of Harvard.* Eugene: University of Oregon Press, 1944.

Jones, Howard M. "Longfellow," in *American Writers on American Literature,* edited by John Macy. New York: Liveright, 1931.

Longfellow, Samuel. *Life of Henry Wadsworth Longfellow.* 2 vols. Boston: Ticknor, 1886.

———. *Final Memorials of Henry Wadsworth Longfellow.* Boston: Ticknor, 1887.

Martin, Ernest. *L'Évangeline de Longfellow et la suite merveilleuse d'un poème.* Paris: Librairie Hachette, 1936.

More, Paul Elmer. "The Centenary of Longfellow," in *Shelburne Essays, Fifth Series.* Boston: Houghton, Mifflin, 1908.

Morin, Paul. *Les Sources de l'Oeuvre de Henry Wadsworth Longfellow.* Paris: Émile Larose, 1913.

O'Neil, Rev. Joseph E., S.J. "Poet of the Feeling Heart," in *American Classics Reconsidered,* edited by Rev. Harold C. Gardiner, S.J. New York: Scribner's, 1958.

Scudder, Horace E. "Longfellow and His Art," in *Men and Books.* Boston: Houghton, Mifflin, 1887.

Thompson, Lawrance. *Young Longfellow, 1807–1843.* New York: Macmillan, 1938.

Van Schaick, John, Jr. *The Characters in "Tales of a Wayside Inn."* Boston: Universalist Publishing House, 1939.

Wagenknecht, Edward. *Longfellow: A Full-Length Portrait.* New York: Longmans, Green, 1955.

———. *Mrs. Longfellow: Selected Letters and Journals of Fanny Appleton.* New York: Longmans, Green, 1956.

Whitman, Iris. *Longfellow and Spain.* New York: Institudo de las Españas en los Estados Unidos, 1927.

Williams, Stanley T. "Longfellow," in Vol. II of *The Spanish Background of American Literature.* 2 vols. New Haven, Conn.: Yale University Press, 1955.